This Grimoire Belongs to

The Wheel of the Year Grimoire

A one year Grimoire to record and reflect on each of the eight festivals of the Pagan Wheel of the Year with festival dates for both northern and southern hemispheres.

Keep this 'Book of the Shadows of things that have been' to record your celebrations and rituals. Being able to look back over the years will help you to plan your current celebrations and allow you to refer back for guidance and ideas.

This one year Grimoire is designed with space to record every aspect of your rituals. It will give you an organized, safe place to keep all your notes and the results of your spell work, rituals and meditations. Having the luxury of keeping a full year of knowledge at your fingertips will allow you to grow in confidence and experience with each successive year.

The Wheel of the Year Grimoire has also been designed as a companion workbook to use with The Wheel of the Year by Maureen Murrish which offers ideas, spells, correspondences and more. By using this Grimoire in conjunction with The Wheel of the Year you will have everything you need to organize and record celebrating eight wonderful and fulfilling festivals.

An' ye harm none, do as ye will.

Blessed Be

Waxing   Full Moon   Waning

Samhain 31 October (1 May) 20__

Location

Members Present

Seasonal Altar Dressing

Tools

Samhain 31 October (1 May) 20__

Correspondences

Deities Invited

Activities

Samhain 31 October (1 May) 20__

Magical Working

Spells Performed / Purpose

Notes

Samhain 31 October (1 May) 20__

Chant

Meditation

Feast

What was my main focus for this festival?

How did I feel during and after it?

What would I change for next year?

_____
_____
_____
_____
_____
_____
_____
_____
_____

What have been the long term effects of my workings?

_____
_____
_____
_____
_____
_____
_____
_____
_____
_____
_____

Waxing   Full Moon   Waning

Yule 20-21 December (21 June) 20__

Location

Members Present

Seasonal Altar Dressing

Tools

Yule 20-21 December (21 June) 20___

Correspondences

Deities Invited

Activities

Yule 20-21 December (21 June) 20___

Magical Working

Spells Performed / Purpose

Notes

Yule 20-21 December (21 June) 20__

Chant

_____
_____
_____
_____
_____

Meditation

_____
_____
_____
_____
_____
_____
_____
_____
_____
_____
_____
_____
_____
_____
_____

Feast

_____
_____
_____
_____
_____
_____
_____

What was my main focus for this festival?

_____

_____

_____

_____

_____

_____

How did I feel during and after it?

_____

_____

_____

_____

_____

_____

_____

_____

_____

_____

_____

_____

_____

What would I change for next year?

_____

_____

_____

_____

_____

_____

_____

_____

What have been the long term effects of my workings?

_____

_____

_____

_____

_____

_____

_____

_____

_____

Waxing   Full Moon   Waning

Imbolc 1-2 February (2 August) 20___

Location

Members Present

Seasonal Altar Dressing

Tools

Imbolc 1-2 February (2 August) 20___

Correspondences

Deities Invited

Activities

Imbolc 1-2 February (2 August) 20__

Magical Working

Spells Performed /Purpose

Notes

Imbolc 1-2 February (2 August) 20__

Chant

Meditation

Feast

What was my main focus for this festival?

_____
_____
_____
_____
_____
_____

How did I feel during and after it?

_____
_____
_____
_____
_____
_____
_____
_____
_____
_____
_____
_____
_____

What would I change for next year?

_____
_____
_____
_____
_____
_____
_____
_____

What have been the long term effects of my workings?

_____
_____
_____
_____
_____
_____
_____
_____
_____
_____
_____
_____

Ostara 20-21 March (21 September) 20__

Location

Members Present

Seasonal Altar Dressing

Tools

Ostara 20-21 March (21 September) 20___

Correspondences

Deities Invited

Activities

Ostara 20-21 March (21 September) 20___

Magical Working

Spells Performed / Purpose

Notes

Ostara 20-21 March (21 September) 20__

Chant

Meditation

Feast

What was my main focus for this festival?

_____
_____
_____
_____
_____
_____
_____

How did I feel during and after it?

_____
_____
_____
_____
_____
_____
_____
_____
_____
_____
_____
_____
_____

What would I change for next year?

_____
_____
_____
_____
_____
_____
_____
_____
_____
_____

What have been the long term effects of my workings?

_____
_____
_____
_____
_____
_____
_____
_____
_____
_____
_____

Waxing   Full Moon   Waning

Beltain 1 May (31 October) 20__

Location

Members Present

Seasonal Altar Dressing

Tools

Beltain 1 May (31 October) 20__

Correspondences

Deities Invited

Activities

Beltain 1 May (31 October) 20__

Magical Working

Spells Performed / Purpose

Notes

Beltain 1 May (31 October) 20__

Chant

Meditation

Feast

What was my main focus for this festival?

_____

_____

_____

_____

_____

_____

How did I feel during and after it?

_____

_____

_____

_____

_____

_____

_____

_____

_____

_____

_____

_____

What would I change for next year?

_____

_____

_____

_____

_____

_____

_____

_____

What have been the long term effects of my workings?

_____

_____

_____

_____

_____

_____

_____

_____

_____

_____

Waxing   Full Moon   Waning

Litha 20-21 June (21 December) 20___

Location

Members Present

Seasonal Altar Dressing

Tools

Litha 20-21 June (21 December) 20___

Correspondences

Deities Invited

Activities

Litha 20-21 June (21 December) 20__

Magical Working

Spells Performed / Purpose

Notes

Litha 20-21 June (21 December) 20__

Chant

Meditation

Feast

What was my main focus for this festival?

_____

_____

_____

_____

_____

How did I feel during and after it?

_____

_____

_____

_____

_____

_____

_____

_____

_____

_____

_____

What would I change for next year?

_____
_____
_____
_____
_____
_____
_____
_____
_____

What have been the long term effects of my workings?

_____
_____
_____
_____
_____
_____
_____
_____
_____

Waxing   Full Moon   Waning

Lammas 1-2 August (2 February) 20__

Location

Members Present

Seasonal Altar Dressing

Tools

Lammas 1-2 August (2 February) 20___

Correspondences

Deities Invited

Activities

Lammas 1-2 August (2 February) 20__

Magical Working

Spells Performed / Purpose

Notes

Lammas 1-2 August (2 February) 20__

Chant

_____
_____
_____
_____
_____

Meditation

_____
_____
_____
_____
_____
_____
_____
_____
_____
_____
_____
_____

Feast

_____
_____
_____
_____
_____
_____
_____

What was my main focus for this festival?

How did I feel during and after it?

What would I change for next year?

_____
_____
_____
_____
_____
_____
_____
_____
_____

What have been the long term effects of my workings?

_____
_____
_____
_____
_____
_____
_____
_____
_____
_____

Mabon 20-21 September (21 March) 20__

Location

Members Present

Seasonal Altar Dressing

Tools

Mabon 20-21 September (21 March) 20__

Correspondences

Deities Invited

Activities

Mabon 20-21 September (21 March) 20__

Magical Working

_____
_____
_____
_____
_____

Spells Performed / Purpose

_____
_____
_____
_____
_____
_____
_____
_____
_____
_____
_____
_____
_____

Notes

_____
_____
_____
_____
_____
_____
_____

Mabon 20-21 September (21 March) 20___

Chant

_____
_____
_____
_____
_____

Meditation

_____
_____
_____
_____
_____
_____
_____
_____
_____
_____
_____
_____
_____
_____

Feast

_____
_____
_____
_____
_____
_____
_____
_____

What was my main focus for this festival?

_____

_____

_____

_____

_____

_____

_____

How did I feel during and after it?

_____

_____

_____

_____

_____

_____

_____

_____

_____

_____

_____

_____

_____

What would I change for next year?

_____

_____

_____

_____

_____

_____

_____

_____

What have been the long term effects of my workings?

_____

_____

_____

_____

_____

_____

_____

_____

_____

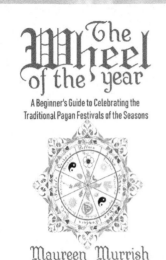

https://maureenmurrish.com

Although this workbook is complete on its own it was designed to complement The Wheel of the Year which is a beginners guide to celebrating the traditional pagan festivals of the seasons. Used together you will have everything you need to celebrate eight wonderful and fulfilling festivals.

Celebrate the ancient and powerful magic held within the Wheel of the Year with this clear and well-ordered guide. This book is much more than a guidebook; it offers everything needed to mark the changing of the seasons in a meaningful and fulfilling way. Within these pages are suggestions for activities, spells, guided meditations and lists of correspondences for each of the eight Sacred Festivals. Learn something of the role of the Goddess and her Consort and gain an understanding of the important role the Festivals played for our ancestors. Also included are guidance on Casting a Circle and collecting and cleansing the basic tools used for Craft work. Although aimed at those new to the Craft it will give the more knowledgeable tried and tested ways to celebrate these ancient and beloved Festivals.

Printed in Great Britain
by Amazon